1 MONTH OF
FREE
READING

at

www.ForgottenBooks.com

By purchasing this book you are eligible for one month membership to ForgottenBooks.com, giving you unlimited access to our entire collection of over 1,000,000 titles via our web site and mobile apps.

To claim your free month visit:
www.forgottenbooks.com/free979367

ISBN 978-0-332-65710-3
PIBN 10979367

For support please visit www.forgottenbooks.com

JUDICIAL SYSTEM

OF

BRITISH INDIA

CONSIDERED WITH ESPECIAL REFERENCE TO THE TRAINING

OF THE

ANGLO-INDIAN JUDGES.

BY AN INDIAN OFFICIAL.

LONDON:

PELHAM RICHARDSON, 23, CORNHILL.

1852.

PELHAM RICHARDSON, PRINTER, 23, CORNHILL.

THE JUDICIAL SYSTEM,

ETC. ETC.

It is satisfactory to observe among the list of subjects submitted for the consideration of the Parliamentary Committees * appointed to report on the affairs of India that the judicial system of that country is one of the topics to which the Committees have been directed to extend their enquiries. It is of much importance that the subject should be thoroughly investigated, for proverbial as is the ignorance and indifference generally manifested by the members of the Legislature on all matters connected with our Indian dependencies, on none, perhaps, does more misconception exist than in regard to the system under which justice is administered in that country to the millions subject to our rule. Nor is it unnatural that a subject of this

* It is proper to state that this pamphlet was written before the dissolution of the late Parliament, and under circumstances which precluded the writer from referring to the minutes of evidence taken before the Committees.

A 2

nature should excite but little interest among the majority of those who usually pay attention to the Parliamentary debates. It is to be expected that to uninitiated ears the very designations of many of the Indian judicial officers should sound fully as repulsive as the technical terms of the laws of our forefathers, which few unprofessional persons pretend to understand, and that to take into consideration the duties of a Court of Sudr Udalut, or to discuss the nature of the training required for a principal Sudr Ameen, should be looked upon by a large number of those who will have to decide upon the various questions affecting the future government of India as being as much out of their proper province as the filing an action for replevin, or drawing out a deed of entail; and the result has been that, notwithstanding the changes which the last twenty years have effected in accelerating and increasing the communication between the mother country and her Indian dominions, on all questions connected with the Indian judicial system the most remarkable ignorance still prevails.

Nor is this want of knowledge confined to our own country. It exists more or less at each of our Indian Presidencies, not only among those of the European residents unconnected with the services, whose avocations confine them to the large Presidency towns, and who have no direct interest in the welfare of the Native population, but among a large majority of the members of the press, whose business it ought to be to make themselves better acquainted with the laws by which the masses of their fellow-subjects are governed, and against which, ignorant as they are of their practical operation, they are ever ready to declaim. It is barely two years since some of the editors of the Calcutta newspapers gravely urged, as a ground for exempting Europeans in the Provinces from the jurisdiction of the criminal Courts of the East India Company, the inhumanities of the Mahomedan Law; implying, if not actually asserting, that the penalties of mutilation prescribed by the Lawgiver of Arabia were to this day recognized by the British Legislature and enforced in their Courts.

From this almost universal ignorance or indifference on the part of persons not actually belonging to the Indian services, as to the plan and principles upon which the administration of justice in that country is conducted, it naturally results that reforms which experience has proved to be most urgently required are left untried, the gross ignorance of the assailants of the existing state of things rendering their attacks comparatively innocuous, and enabling the authorities year after year to lull themselves in the delusion that, because on some points the evils of the system are much misrepresented and exaggerated, therefore they exist only in the imaginations of those who denounce them.

If we are to put any faith in the sweeping accusations which so constantly appear in the columns

of the Indian newspapers, the Company's Judges
are as a body utterly inefficient, and if not themselves actually corrupt, yet so entirely dependent
upon the Native officials in their Courts, and such
mere puppets in their hands, as to render it, in
point of fact, a matter of indifference to the suitors
whether the perversion of justice, which is of daily
occurrence, is to be traced no further than the
ministerial subordinates or to the Bench of Justice
itself. The knowledge of the language in which
the proceedings are conducted, if possessed by the
presiding Judge, is to all intents and purposes
useless. His knowledge of the people, his experience of the Native character, the powers with
which nature may have endowed him of distinguishing between truth and falsehood, the aptitude for
business which he may be supposed to have acquired
from long practice in official duties,—all are utterly
paralysed by the overweening influence of the clerk
who records the depositions of the witnesses, or of
the Serishtadar who files the pleadings of the parties
in a suit. In the Court over which he presides
justice is a mere mockery, the redress of grievances
a mere matter of purchase; and even then, in many
instances, so delayed as to make it problematical
whether it be not to the advantage of the suitor to
submit patiently to the original wrong, rather than
to subject himself to the expenditure of time and
money which a resort to the Court must inevitably
entail. In the trial of criminal cases the incom-

petency of the Bench is no less remarkable, and what with the over-scrupulousness and timidity of some Judges, and the unscrupulousness and ignorance of others, either the exertions of the magistracy to repress crime are entirely foiled, or the lives and liberties of the innocent are imperilled to an extent without comparison under other civilized Governments.

Such is the state of our Indian judicial system if we are to believe the representations which not unfrequently appear in the local journals, and are really received by a large portion of the public as if fully founded on fact.

If, on the other hand, we are to rely on the statements of the upholders of the existing system, the Judges are as a body most thoroughly efficient, well versed in the languages, the customs, the feelings, the character, and the laws of the people, and from the experience they have acquired by their previous training in the Revenue and Magisterial Departments, are on the whole not only well fitted for their posts, but literally the only class of men in whom, having reference to the circumstances of the country, the several requisites for the due discharge of judicial functions are to be found combined. The majority of the suits which come before them involve questions of the tenure of land or claims for the recovery of simple debts, for the decision of which they are pre-eminently fitted by their previous practical experience in the administration of the

land revenue, and by the opportunities they have
enjoyed of acquiring an insight into the character of
the Natives, and of familiarity with their habits and
customs, when so engaged. An acquaintance with
the principles of the English Law is altogether
unnecessary and by no means to be desired. Local
experience aided by sound common sense enables
them in the majority of cases to decide correctly,
and is far more valuable than any other training of
a more strictly professional kind. For the trial
of criminals they are equally fitted by their previous preparation as magistrates, and by the
remarkable power of appreciating evidence and dis-
criminating between truth and falsehood, which can
only be acquired in the cutcherry of the assistant-
magistrate and in the revenue officer's tent. As
to the alleged influence of the ministerial officers of
the Courts and the perversion of justice which
thence ensues, it is a mere fiction, originating in the
minds of those who proclaim it, and as unfounded
in fact as it is opposed to reason ; the experience of
the Judges and their knowledge of the language in
which business is conducted, rendering it impossible
that they should be imposed upon by those whose
duty it is to carry out their orders, and whose functions are purely ministerial. It is true that bribes
and presents are very frequently given, and in some
localities are supposed to be a necessary preliminary
to obtaining legal address; but this is entirely at-
tributable to the moral consideration of the Natives

themselves. They see nothing disgraceful in the practice, and when offences of this kind are charged against the Court servants by disappointed suitors, the difficulties of proving them are so great in consequence of the secret manner in which the transaction has taken place, that they are seldom followed by conviction and punishment, and the suitors remain blind to the utter worthlessness of the supposed influence for which they have so largely paid. The evil is of the people's own creation and cannot be charged against the Judges, who do all in their power to counteract it. No other class of men could perform more efficiently the duties entrusted to them. It seems doubtful whether a more strictly professional education would not be found productive of evils which do not at present exist.

Such is the language commonly used in defence of the existing system. Such, without exaggeration, are the arguments of the majority of Indian officials, acted on, it must be presumed, by the authorities in this country, and so furnishing an explanation of the tardiness of reform, and of the expenditure of money and labour involved in the establishment of the Indian Law Commission having been attended with such unsatisfactory results. Less preposterous, certainly, than the wholesale accusations we have already referred to, but more really prejudicial to the public interests, inasmuch as they wear a certain appearance of plausibility, and so are calculated to obstruct the progress of necessary reform, and to perpetuate the continuance of evils the existence of which they deny.

The truth is that neither of the foregoing descriptions presents by any means a correct picture of the real state of things they purport to describe. It would be equally incorrect to imagine that the Courts are in the state of utter inefficiency alleged by the one party, as to suppose that as a general rule the Judges are as well fitted for their duties as is asserted by the other. That many of the Company's Courts are well and ably presided over, it would be impossible to deny ; but at the same time it must be admitted that much room for improvement exists, and that, when viewed as a system, the judicial administration is in a less satisfactory condition than most of the other departments of the State. The increase of late years in the number of Courts presided over by Native Judges has been attended in many respects with very beneficial results, especially as regards the more speedy administration of justice in civil suits ; and the system of employing native industry and intelligence in the primary disposal of suits under the safeguard of an immediate appeal to the European functionaries is undoubtedly based upon sound and politic principles ; but in carrying it into practice a serious evil has been experienced, in the diminished opportunities which now exist for affording the necessary previous training to the Judges of the Appellate Courts.

It is the object of the following pages to furnish
an impartial sketch of the merits and demerits of
the existing system, and of the measures which we
conceive to be necessary to place it upon an efficient footing; and if it be our " duty to atone to
" the people of India for the sufferings they en-
" dured and the wrongs to which they were ex-
" posed in being reduced to our rule, and to afford
" them such advantages and confer on them such
" benefits as may in some degree console them for
" the loss of their independence,"* surely in no
department of the Government is the recognition
of this duty more imperative than in the administration of the Law, upon the efficiency of which
the security of person and property so entirely
depends. It is an easy matter to institute a comparison between the vices and oppressions of the
Mahomedan princes, and the beneficence and purity
of the British rule. The contrast, no doubt, is
satisfactory to the philanthropist, though frequently
much exaggerated, especially as regards the result.
It is necessary that the British Government should
go further than this, and before halting in the course
of reform, be able to assure itself that it has done
its utmost so to organize its administration in all its
departments as to render it conducive to the hap-
piness and welfare of the millions whom Providence
has entrusted to its charge.

* Extract from a Speech of Sir R. Peel.

Confining ourselves, then,
ment, the immediate subject
be well to premise the sugg
to offer in regard to it by
Courts as they are at present
be a task exceeding the limit
trace their history from thei
and it will be sufficient for tl
describe the existing state of
the several Courts are con
extent of their respective jur
ture of the training undergo
preside in them.

In the large Presidency
Madras, and Bombay, the adi
is conducted by Courts establ
ter, whose jurisdiction, exce
European British subjects, is
dents within certain very r
does not, it is believed, exten
tance of seven miles from t
the civil department these C
current jurisdiction with the
pany in taking cognizance
against European British sub
the Company's territories. In
ment their jurisdiction is mor
nizance of all civil crimes cor
British subjects throughout In
restricted to them.

In addition to the Queen's Courts, there is likewise at each of the three superior Presidencies, as well as at Agra, the capital of the north-west Provinces, a chief Company's Court, called the Sudder Court, which is not only the highest Court of Appeal from all sentences and decrees and orders passed by the Courts in the Provinces, but is vested with an executive superintendence over all the lower Courts, and tries in the last resort certain criminal cases, the records of which, subject to certain rules, which will be presently adverted to, are referred to it by the lower Courts for decision.

In the Sudder Court at Calcutta there are five Judges, in that at Agra three, at Madras three, and at Bombay four. At the two latter Presidencies one of the members of Council is ex-officio Chief Judge of the Sudder Court, but his duties as such are almost nominal, and except when called in on special occasions he takes no part in the proceedings of the Court.

The Judges of these Courts are all appointed from the higher ranks of the Civil Service, and are usually taken from the judicial branch of it, but not invariably; several instances being on record of officers with little or no judicial experience being removed direct from a revenue office to the Sudder Bench. These anomalies, however, are of rare occurrence, and the selection may now be said to be practically confined to the Courts. The rule of seniority, by which the promotion in the Civil

Service is regulated to a considerable extent, is supposed to be discarded in the appointments to the Sudder Court, but practically much weight is attached to it, and the Bench is too often filled by men whose energies are nearly expended, and whose capacities would at no time have entitled them to such a responsible post. It is to be borne in mind that in addition to the high and arduous duties devolving upon these Courts as the highest Courts of Appeal, and as the Courts of last resort in criminal cases, the general superintendence exercised by them over the judicial functionaries in the Provinces renders it of the utmost importance to the maintenance of a correct and uniform course of procedure throughout the country, that the Judges who preside in them should be officers of superior qualifications. The principle, however, does not appear to be practically recognized by the Indian Governments, for from a recent work* which contains much useful information regarding the Indian administration in its several departments, we learn that " the Sudder Courts are generally composed " of men much too old to commence an useful " career ;" and that " it is but very recently that the " Lieutenant-Governor" (of Agra, it is presumed " is intended) " has perpetrated the innovation of " putting some of the youngest and best Judges " into the Sudder :" and if we may judge from cer-

---

* Modern India, by George Campbell, Bengal Civil Service.

tain proceedings in the Sudder Court at Madras which came before the public during the government of the Marquis of Tweeddale, it would seem that at that Presidency up to no very distant period other claims were attended to in the selection of the Judges than those of superior efficiency and fitness for high judicial office.

The judicial functions of the Sudder Courts comprise the hearing of appeals from the decrees and orders of the Civil Courts in the Provinces, and of applications for the admission of special appeals from the decisions of those Courts, when exercising an appellate jurisdiction, such special appeals being admissible only in those cases in which the decision of the lower Court may be shewn to be defective in some point of law, or of practice having the force of law.

For the reversal of any decree or order of a lower Court the concurrence of two Judges of the Sudder Court is required, it being competent to a single Judge, if approving of the decree or order appealed from, to confirm the same without reference to his colleagues.

An appeal lies to Her Majesty in Council from the decree and order of the Sudder Courts, provided the value of the matter litigated exceed 10,000 rupees, or £1000.

In the criminal department it is the province of the Sudder Courts to pass sentence in all cases of murder, treason, or rebellion belonging to gangs of Thugs, Suttee, and rape, as well as all cases of robbery by open violence (or as it is termed in Bengal, " Dacoity "), in which a sentence of fourteen years imprisonment with corporal punishment may be considered insufficient by the Judge presiding at the trial; as also in all other cases in which the presiding Judge may differ from the Futwa (or opinion) of his Mahomedan law officer, or from the verdict of the assessor or jury associated with him on the trial in regard to the sufficiency or insufficiency of the evidence for the conviction of the accused.

In all these cases a complete copy or translation of the record is forwarded to the Sudder Court with the opinion of the presiding Judge as to the merits of the case, and, if it be for conviction, with a recommendation as to the punishment to be adjudged; and on perusal of the record the Sudder Court passes sentence and orders it to be carried out by the lower Court.

The peculiarity of the system is this :—that for all the more serious offences the sentence is passed by a Court which has not had the advantage of hearing the evidence as it was actually delivered, and is therefore without those important aids to its due appreciation, which are afforded by observing the demeanor of the witnesses, and which so frequently enable a Judge or jury to satisfy themselves as to their credibility from the manner in which their answers are given.

It follows as an obvious result that evidence is very frequently rejected by the higher Court, which, if the examination of the witness had taken place before it, would have been fully credited, and the course of justice is thus considerably obstructed by the erroneous acquittals which ensue; but, though an evil, it seems to be a necessary one under the existing system, and far preferable to the alternative of vesting powers of life and death in Judges appointed upon the principles which in many cases regulate the selection of the officers who preside in the local Session Courts.

Various remedies have been suggested, and among others that of deputing the Sudder Judges to hold periodical circuits for the trial of the more serious crimes; but the delays in the jail deliveries which such a measure would entail, unless the number of the Judges were considerably increased, would form an insuperable objection to its adoption.

Of all criminal cases disposed of by the lower Courts without reference, abstract statements are forwarded to the Sudder Court, upon perusal of which, as also upon petition from prisoners, it is competent to the latter Court to confirm, modify, or reverse the sentence as it may see fit.

Next in rank to the Sudder Courts at the Presidencies are the local Civil and Session Courts, one of which is located in each district, presided over by a single Judge, selected, as the Sudder Judges, from the ranks of the Civil Service.

In the appointments of these officers at all
the Presidencies seniority would seem to be the
established rule, the rules of the Service being
apparently considered to preclude any attempt at
selection on account of superior ability or of
superior qualifications for the judicial office.

Of the system in Bengal, where the Civil and
Session Judges have no preparatory judicial training
whatever, the author of the work already quoted
writes as follows:—

" When a collector is old enough he is made
" a Judge; and to this step there is almost no
" exception if it is wished for. It seems to be
" considered that if at this time of life a man
" is fit for anything at all he is fit to be a Judge;
" and if he is fit for nothing better, make him
" a Judge and get rid of him, for once in that
" office he has no claim to further promotion by
" seniority alone. The judicial department being
" in a less satisfactory state than any other is less
" sought after, and the ill effects of mismanagement
" being less immediately startling, the principle
" that (in a choice of evils) any man will do
" for a Judge seems to have become established.
" Some who mismanage their districts are said
" to be promoted to be Judges against their will.
" Moreover, all who can get anything out of the
" regular hire have by this time got it. A crack
" magistrate and collector probably prefers a com-
" missionership in the Punjab, or to wait for one

" in the Provinces; and men are now nearly
" entitled to their pensions before they get judge-
" ships. Altogether it happens that comparatively
" few much above mediocrity remain to be Judges;
" and of those who do, many are disappointed
" and many hang on when they are old and worn
" out. A bad department is then made worse."

We have not sufficient information to enable us to
state whether a similar system prevails in Bombay,
but there, as in Madras and in the North-West
Provinces, the offices of collector and magistrate
are united in one person; and in the two former
Presidencies there is a subordinate grade of Judgeships filled by members of the Civil Service, which
are intended to afford a preparatory training for the
higher Courts.

At Madras, however, the principle adverted to by
Mr. Campbell, that " *any man will do for a Judge*,"
has long been the established rule, and notwithstanding the advantages afforded by the existence
of the subordinate Judgeships, the higher appointments are not unfrequently bestowed upon revenue
officers who have proved themselves wanting in
efficiency, and are considered unfit for a responsible
revenue charge. To such an extent has this mis-
direction of patronage been carried for many years
past that the judicial line is commonly talked of as
" the refuge for the destitute " at Madras.

At first sight it is difficult to understand how such
a system could ever have been permitted to exist,

still more so how it should have been tolerated as it
has been for a considerable number of years. It
seems so obvious that upon the efficiency of the
Courts of Justice the security of person and property must very materially depend, and that by their
inefficiency the objects of good government must be
neutralized to a very considerable extent. It is necessary, however, to view the question with a due regard
to the peculiar circumstances of the country, and
it then becomes more apparent why the judicial
department should so long have been treated as a
comparatively unimportant department of the State.
In India the Government revenue is derived almost
entirely from the land. The system of collection is
somewhat a complicated one, and from the nature of
the climate and the habits and condition of the inhabitants it is absolutely requisite, not only for the
realization of the Government dues, but for the
prosperity of the people, that its administration
should be entrusted to able hands. It follows not
unnaturally that the incompetency of a revenue
officer, which must so directly affect the interests not
only of the governing but of the governed, should
have been considered by all Indian Governments of
far more importance than inefficiency in a Judge,
whose decisions, if erroneous, bear less directly upon
the mass of the population, though probably not less
injurious in their eventual results. Reference has
already been made to the rule of seniority in the
Civil Service, upon which so much stress has inva-

riably been laid by the Home authorities that it has been almost impossible for the local Government to depart from it in any considerable degree. This rule, which was laid down avowedly for the purpose of preventing any undue favoritism or jobbery in the distribution of the Government patronage, and was probably more applicable to the condition and circumstances of the service when it was originally proposed than it is to the existing state of things, has hitherto been more strictly adhered to in the judicial department than in any other branch, and for the same reasons which have led to the comparative unimportance hitherto attached to it.

Of late years, however, marked symptoms of improvement have been manifested, and in the increased publicity which has been afforded to the proceedings of the Courts presided over by European functionaries by the publication of their decrees and of reports of the criminal cases tried by them, a step in advance has been taken which cannot fail to lead to other improvements, and the beneficial effects of which are already beginning to be felt.

The Civil and Session Judges in Bengal and Madras in their capacity of Civil Judges have a primary jurisdiction in all suits of whatever value; and all suits wherein the value of the property in litigation may exceed in Bengal rupees 5000 or £500, and Madras rupees 10,000 or £1000, must of necessity be instituted in their Courts; though in Bengal it is competent to and is the practice of the

Civil Judges to refer all suits of whatever amount
for trial by the principal Sudder Ameens.

The number, however, of original suits instituted
in the Courts of the Civil Judges in these Presidencies is comparatively trifling, and practically
their civil duties are confined almost entirely to the
hearing of appeals from the decrees and orders of
the inferior Courts.

In Bombay the civil functions of the Zillah Judges
are with a trifling exception (with reference to suits
in which the Government is a defendant) confined
exclusively to appeals.

In the criminal department in their capacity of
Session Judge they hold permanent sessions for the
trial of all cases committed by the subordinate
functionaries entrusted with the primary investigation. In Bengal and Madras a Mahomedan law-
officer is attached to each Session Court, whose
duty it is to sit with the Session Judge at the trial,
and at the conclusion thereof to deliver his Futwa
or opinion in regard to the sufficiency or insufficiency of the evidence for the conviction of the
accused ; stating fully the grounds of his judgment,
and in case of conviction the nature of the punishment to which the prisoner is liable under the Mahomedan Law. The Judge, if he concurs in the
Futwa, either releases the prisoner, or, if the
offence charged be within his competency to dispose
of, passes sentence according to law. In the Bombay Courts all reference to the Mahomedan Law

has been long since abrogated, and the penal la
of that Presidency is nearly all contained in oɪ
extensive Regulation enacted in 1827. The Sessic
Judges in Bombay, as well as the more subordinat
judicial officers, have the power of calling iι
Natives to sit with them as assessors in the trial o
both civil and criminal cases, but this discretionarɣ
power seems to be rarely exercised.

The employment of assessors in lieu of the Mahomedan law-officer in criminal trials held before
the Session Courts has been sanctioned by the
legislature both in Bengal and Madras, and in the
former Presidency, we believe, is now resorted to
to a considerable extent.

The practice does not seem to have been hitherto
very generally adopted in Madras.

The severest sentence it is competent to the Session Courts to pass without reference to the Sudder
is in Bengal, sixteen years imprisonment with hard
labour in irons, and in Madras, fourteen years imprisonment, and corporal punishment to the extent
of 195 lashes with a cat-o'-nine tails. In the Bombay Courts the sentence in every case is *passed* by
the Court of Session, subject, however, to the confirmation of the Sudder Court if the punishment
exceed imprisonment for seven years.

It will be proper in this place to explain briefly
the nature of the reference now made to the Mahomedan Law in the administration of criminal justice in the Bengal and Madras Presidencies, where,

in form at least, it is still recognized to a certain extent. Some explanation on this point is necessary, as it has been very recently urged as one of the principal grounds for continuing to British subjects the exemption they at present enjoy from the criminal jurisdiction of the Mofussil Courts. The Mahomedan Criminal Law, it is to be observed, was that in force throughout the greater portion of the present British Indian territories when the country came under our rule; and as it was the policy of the Company, upon the first acquisition of the Government, to retain and gradually to modify the system of criminal jurisprudence which it found established, the Mahomedan Law continued to be for some time the basis of all penal enactments passed by the Anglo-Indian Legislature. It was in fact recognized as the criminal " lex loci," but so modified in certain points as to render its operations not inconsistent with European notions as to the nature of the penalties to be inflicted for crime. All punishments, therefore, involving mutilation were abolished at the outset,* and when de-

---

* When it is said that the infliction of such penalties was proscribed " *from the outset*," reference of course is made to the earliest legislative enactments; but when it is borne in mind that the earliest of the laws of the Madras Presidency were not passed until 1802, it becomes obvious that the administration of justice must frequently have been conducted, for a considerable period after the establishment of our Government, upon principles very repugnant to those which would be tolerated in the present day. A

clared by the law officers as prescribed by law for the crime proved, were to be commuted to imprisonment for certain specified periods according to the nature of the penalty denounced.

curious illustration of the state of things existing previous to that period is afforded in the subjoined correspondence between an officer of considerable reputation engaged in the management of a newly-acquired district, and the Board of Revenue at Madras.

To the President and Members of the Board of Revenue, Fort St. George.

GENTLEMEN,

(The four first paragraphs have reference to Revenue matters.)

Par. 5. I am sorry to acquaint you there have been three murders and many robberies committed in these districts of late, especially in the Baramahal. The inhabitants of Woomaloor cheerfully entered into engagements to make restitution of all effects stolen in their district, but those in the Baramahal object to it, on account of their being surrounded by hills and polygars, which may make it necessary to appoint cavillagars. If you approve of my appointing them, please to inform me of the mode to be adopted for their support. It might be done by a resoom on ploughs or houses, which might be collected by the servants of the sirkar.

Par. 6. As immediate and severe example should be made of such robbers as may be apprehended, I request to be informed what judicial authority is annexed to my station as collector.

Par. 7. I punished one man of a gang lately convicted of driving off the inhabitants' cattle several times to the other side of the Canvery, *by depriving him of his ears,* and have now four in custody accused of murders, which from every appearance they have committed.

I have the honor to be, Gentlemen,

Your obedient servant,

(Signed)   A. READ,

Salem, 27th July, 1792.   *Collector.*

But although the inhumanities of the Mahomedan Law were proscribed from the beginning, its rules of evidence, so replete with ridiculous technicalities, and consequently so calculated to facilitate the escape of the guilty, continued for several years to be practically in force in the Anglo-Indian Courts; and it was not until 1818 that the Sudder Court at Madras was empowered to overrule acquittals by its Mahomedan law-officers, while the Judges of circuit in that Presidency, whose functions correspond with those now possessed by the Session Judges, were compelled, until so late as 1829, to refer every case

No. LXIX.

To Captain ALEXANDER READ,
> *Collector in the district of Baramahal and Salem.*

Par. 4. With regard to the punishment you inflicted as represented in your letter of the 27th ultimo by depriving a man of his ears, the Board as well as Government, to whom the circumstance has been stated, are perfectly assured you was actuated in this proceeding by the sincere belief that such an example of severity would be attended with good effect, but as punishments of this nature are totally irreconcileable with the principle and practice of our Government, you are forbidden to inflict them in any instance of guilt however atrocious, and until regular Courts of justice can be established, persons accused of great offences must be confined until they can be brought to regular trial. Smaller offences may be punished by fine, imprisonment, or whipping, agreeably to existing regulations, but in no other manner whatever.

I am, Sir,
Your most obedient servant,
(Signed)   WILLIAM HARINGTON.
Fort St. George, 17th August, 1792.

for the final judgment of the Sudder Court, in which, though the proof of guilt appeared sufficient, the evidence was rejected by the Mahomedan law-officer upon purely technical grounds.

Under an enactment passed in the latter year, all personal objections taken by the Mahomedan law-officers in their Futwas to the evidence of prosecutors or witnesses, on the ground of their testimony being inadmissible under the rules of the Mahomedan Law, as, for instance, that they are persons not of the Mahomedan persuasion, &c., the Session Judges are empowered to remove by a second question, propounded to ascertain to what penalties the accused would have been liable in the absence of the personal objections advanced to the evidence of those witnesses whose testimony. may have been pronounced inadmissible, and then to pass sentence according to law.

The result has been that, so far as it is found compatible with the existing state of things in India, the English law of evidence is now the guide of the Courts in the trial of criminal cases, and we find it stated in a letter from the Madras Sudder Court to the Government of that Presidency dated so far back as the 28th May, 1829, that by the provisions of Regulation I. of 1818 the Court considered itself released from the obligation of observing the Mahomedan law of evidence, and that it had accordingly " turned to the law of England as its legitimate " guide, and as the acknowledged source of the

" provisions previously enacted in the Regulations
" of this Government for the conduct of judicial
" procedure."

It is manifest, therefore, that the rules of the
Mahomedan Law, though originally the basis upon
which the laws of the several Indian Presidencies
were founded, have with the progress of legislation
been gradually departed from, and that, whatever
reference is now made to them in the adjudication
of penal sentences, is rather a form than a reality;
the part taken by the Mahomedan law-officers when
associated with the Session Judges in the trial of
criminal cases being to all intents and purposes
that of assessors rather than of expounders of
the law.

It is true that there is a large class of cases
for which no specific penalties are laid down in
the enactments of the Legislature, but which,
being punishable under the Mahomedan Law,
are declared cognizable by the officers of the
magistracy and the Courts, and punishable by
them according to their discretion within certain
prescribed limits.

It is true, also, that the provisions of the law
under which such a discretionary power is vested
in the Courts of taking cognizance of offences,
merely on the ground that they are pronounced
punishable by the Mahomedan Law, are liable to
the objection that some acts are declared punishable
under that Law which, according to European

principles of criminal jurisprudence, are not treated as penal offences, and that British subjects, if amenable to the jurisdiction of the Company's tribunals, might be subjected to imprisonment for acts which by the laws of their native country are not cognizable by the criminal Courts.

In theory this is certainly an objection, and one of which the so-called Anti-Black Act agitators at Calcutta were fully entitled to avail themselves, when on a recent occasion appealing against the proposed removal of their immunity from the jurisdiction of the Company's Courts; but though an objection, it scarcely seems entitled to the weight which has been hitherto attached to it, or to be compared to the public inconvenience, which so frequently results from the exemption of one particular class of persons from the established Courts of the country, and the necessity which is consequently imposed upon prosecutors and witnesses of travelling several hundred miles in order that the offender may be tried by the laws of the land of his birth, instead of being subjected to those in force in the country in which he has thought fit to settle; and considered in this point of view, the exemption referred to appears to us to have been justly pronounced a crying grievance and evil, " entirely incompatible with the freedom " to reside in the country and to carry on all " dealings now accorded " to the class of persons adverted to. It is at the same time perfectly natural that they should be unwilling to have their lives and liberties placed at the mercy of incompetent tribunals, which was another of the grounds of objection urged by them, and which, if founded on fact, (as is to be feared must be admitted to a certain extent,) while it is entitled to far more consideration than any exceptions that may be taken to the system of law at present in force, affords at the same time conclusive evidence of the necessity for an improvement in the system under which the Courts are filled. It is surely somewhat inconsistent with those principles of toleration and equal justice between persons of all creeds, colours, and castes, which are so constantly proclaimed by the Anglo-Indian Government, that Courts considered not sufficiently efficient for the trial of British criminals should be vested with powers of life and death over the millions of the native population, and that the latter should further be subjected to the very serious hardship and inconvenience of leaving their distant homes, and of repairing to the Queen's Courts at the Presidency in the capacity of prosecutors and witnesses, whenever a British subject settled among the mmay think fit to violate the law. Considering the public inconvenience and expense which is likewise entailed, and weighing in the balance the arguments that may be adduced on the other side, founded on the so-called indefeasible rights of free-born Britons to be tried by their own laws in every quarter of the globe, every principle of justice demands that such an anomaly should no longer be permitted to continue. Every consideration satisfies us that the reforms which its removal will necessitate cannot fail to be attended with the most beneficial results.

It is time to resume the sketch of the constitution of the Courts. It has been shown that in all the Presidencies the Civil and Session Courts, so far as regards their jurisdiction and powers, are very much on a par. In regard to the inferior tribunals there is more dissimilarity, although the general principles upon which they are constituted at the different Presidencies are very much the same. In Bengal the judicial authority immediately below that of the Civil and Session Court is divided between two officers, of whom the one, under the designation of Principal Sudder Ameen, is almost entirely restricted to civil duties; the administration of criminal justice in cases below the jurisdiction of the Session Court being vested in the magistrate, who, in addition to his duties as committing officer, in all cases committable to the Court of Sessions, and as superintendent of the police in the district under his charge, has certain judicial powers in criminal cases to the extent of three years imprisonment in cases of theft and burglary, and of two years imprisonment in cases of affrays.

The Principal Sudder Ameens have an ordinary original jurisdiction in civil suits up to 5000 rupees, or £500, but can try any suits referred to them by the Civil Courts irrespectively of their amount or value.

Next in rank to the Principal Sudder Ameens are the Sudder Ameens, who try suits up to 1000 rupees, or £100; and last come the District Moonsiffs, whose jurisdiction is limited to claims not exceeding in amount or value the sum of 300 rupees, or £30.

Of the above-mentioned functionaries the magistrates and their assistants are invariably officers of the covenanted Civil Service; the Principal Sudder Ameens, Sudder Ameens, and Moonsiffs being mostly natives, and all of them uncovenanted officers. There is likewise a grade of deputy magistrates, who are also uncovenanted officers.

In Madras at most of the Zillah Court Stations there is an inferior Court next to the Civil and Session Court, presided over by an officer, who, if a member of the Civil Service, is designated as Subordinate Judge; if not a covenanted officer, as Principal Sudder Ameen. These subordinate Courts try original suits to the amount of 10,000 rupees, or £1000, and appeal suits to any amount, if referred to them by the Civil Judge.

In the criminal department their powers extend to two years imprisonment, and corporal punishment to the extent of 150 lashes with a cat-o'-nine-tails in cases of theft and burglary; while all other cases for which a more severe punishment than six months imprisonment with corporal punishment to the extent above-mentioned, or with a fine of 200 rupees, may not have been expressly prescribed, they are authorized to dispose of by a sentence to that extent, the infliction of corporal punishment being restricted to cases of theft.

The miscellaneous cases thus provided for embrace, as well as theft, all those offences against the law which are usually designated as misdemeanors; and in respect of *them* the officers of the magistracy in the Madras Presidency exercise a concurrent jurisdiction with the subordinate Courts.

With a few special exceptions, all cases tried by the latter tribunals must have been committed for trial by an officer of the magistracy or of the native police. In cases cognizable by the Courts of Session the functions of the subordinate Court are somewhat analogous to those of a grand jury, it being for the Sub-Judge to decide whether the evidence forwarded by the magistracy or police, if confirmed before him by the deponents, is sufficient to justify the accused being put upon his trial with a reasonable probability of conviction.

The Sudder Ameens in the Madras Presidency, one of whom is invariably the Mahomedan law-officer of the Session Court, try suits up to 2500 rupees, or £250, and are likewise invested with a criminal jurisdiction concurrent with that exercised

c

by the subordinate Courts in cases referred to them by the latter tribunal for trial.

The District Moonsiffs, as in Bengal, have no criminal jurisdiction, but try suits up to 1000 rupees, or £100.

The officers of the magistracy, all of whom in Madras are taken exclusively from the covenanted Civil Service, exercise, as has been already stated, a concurrent jurisdiction with the subordinate criminal Courts in the trial of thefts and misdemeanors, their powers of punishment extending to six months imprisonment with fine or corporal punishment; the fine, if not paid, being commutable to additional imprisonment for six months. They have also more limited powers in the disposal of petty misdemeanors and petty thefts, in which cases a certain limited judicial authority is vested in the native heads of district police and of village police; and the last mentioned officers have in addition a civil jurisdiction in the trial of suits for money or personal property not exceeding ten rupees or £1.

In Bombay the original jurisdiction in civil matters is confined almost entirely to the native tribunals; that of the Principal Sudder Ameen being unlimited, while the jurisdiction of the Sudder Ameen extends to 10,000 rupees, or £1000; and that of the District Moonsiffs to 5000 rupees, or £500. Next in rank to the Civil and Session Judges there is in Bombay a grade of assistant

Judgeships, filled, as the subordinate Judgeships in
Madras, by members of the Civil Service whose
civil duties, like those of the Civil Judges, appear
to be almost exclusively appellate.

In Bombay as in Madras the office of collector
and magistrate is united, and that officer in his
magisterial capacity exercises a criminal jurisdiction to the extent of one year's imprisonment. His
assistants (who as well as himself are members of
the covenanted Civil Service) exercise a similar
jurisdiction, with this restriction,—that in all cases
in which their sentences may exceed three months
imprisonment, they require to be confirmed by the
magistrate before being carried out.

All cases beyond the jurisdiction of the magistracy are committed to the Session Court, except
at certain stations, at which there are detached
Assistant Session Judges, to whom they are committed direct, and either tried by them if the offence
charged be within their jurisdiction, or committed
for trial by the Session Judge of the district, who
proceeds twice a-year to such detached stations to
deliver the gaol.

The powers of punishment of the Assistant Session Judges extend to two years imprisonment, and
in some instances to seven years; all sentences
passed by them in excess of two years being subject
to confirmation by the Session Judge.

The native judicial officers of the Bombay Presidency have no criminal jurisdiction whatever.

It will be observed, from the foregoing sketch of the Courts as they are at present constituted, that the inferior tribunals in the different Presidencies differ considerably as to the extent of their powers and jurisdiction. While in Bengal the limit of the District Moonsiffs' jurisdiction is 300 rupees or £30, in Madras it extends to 1000 rupees, and in Bombay to 5000 rupees. In Bengal* and Bombay (if we except the class of deputy-magistrates in the former Presidency) the functions of the uncovenanted judicial officers are almost entirely confined to the civil department; whereas in Madras all but the District Moonsiffs exercise a criminal jurisdiction. Madras, again, is the only one of the Presidencies in which the covenanted officers have any opportunity of exercising an original jurisdiction in the trial of civil suits, so obviously essential as a preparatory training for the functions of a Court of Appeal. In Bengal there is not a single situation in the civil branch of the judicial department open to a member of the Civil Service before his elevation to the office of Civil and Session Judge; and as regards the criminal branch in the latter Presidency, we learn from a report of the Law Commissioners dated in 1842, since which period but few changes have been effected in the Bengal judicial system, that

---

* In Bengal the Principal Sudder Ameens are competent to pass sentence as far as one month's imprisonment for petty misdemeanours and thefts referred to them by the magistrate for disposal.

although " those civil servants who have risen
" through the grades of assistant, joint-magistrate,
" and magistrate have the benefit of the knowledge
" and experience acquired in those offices when
" called to exercise the powers of a Session Judge ;"
yet that in Bengal Proper " such a preparation is
" not considered indispensable, and an officer con-
" versant only in revenue matters is equally eligible
" to that appointment."

This brings us to the question of training, and
especially to that of the covenanted Judges who
preside in the Courts of Appeal, and upon whose
efficiency the well-working of the entire system
must so materially depend ; and it must be con-
fessed that the training which does take place, if,
indeed, it may be called such, is most sadly defective. It is true that at Haileybury the future civilian is afforded an opportunity of acquiring a knowledge of the first principles of jurisprudence, but
from the number of subjects embraced in the course
of instruction at that institution, and the greater
stress laid upon the study of the Oriental languages,
the number of those who derive any real benefit
from the lectures of the Law Professor is but small.
Mr. Campbell informs us in the work already quoted,
that the " regulations of the College have been too
" much in the hands of admirers of the Oriental
" languages ;" and that " the distinguishing feature
" of the whole system there is this :—that while
" the study of the Oriental languages is compulsory,

" that of the other, or what are called European
" subjects, is in practice purely voluntary ;" and as
an instance of the working of the system he adduces
the case of a cotemporary of his own, who at his
final examination was passed and reported qualified
for the public service, " having been *publicly*
" assigned by *each* and *every* professor of European
" subjects the mark which in one Oriental would
" have plucked him—that of ' little,' which being
interpreted means ' nothing.'" This is clearly an
extreme case, and it is within the writer's knowledge, that of late years a certain standard of proficiency in the European subjects has been made
requisite for the attainment of the final certificate ;
and the attendance at the law lectures, which
formerly was not enforced until the second half-year
after the student's admission into the College, is
now required throughout the whole of the colle-
giate course. But though the picture drawn by
Mr. Campbell of the system at Haileybury is somewhat exaggerated, the conclusions to be drawn from
it are certainly more correct than those which might
be deduced from observations not long since made
by Lord Brougham in his place in Parliament regarding the education of the officers entrusted with
the duty of presiding in the Courts of the East
India Company. " The Judges of the Native
Courts," observed his lordship, (meaning thereby
the Courts of the Company in contradistinction to
the Crown Courts,) " are obtained from the Civil

" Service of the Company ; and the young men at
" Haileybury who go out as writers are qualified to
" exercise these responsible functions by being
" carefully educated at Haileybury by the most
" learned professors, among whom I may mention
" Dr. Empson, the Professor of Law, and my ex-
" cellent friend Mr. Jones, the Professor of History
" and Political Economy. Here these young
" gentlemen to the number of eighty or ninety are
" being instructed in law, in history, in the Ori-
" ental languages, and every thing that can fit
" them for the discharge of their future duties.
" And this institution is a gratifying proof of the
" great improvement effected during the last twenty-
" five years in the Judges of the East India Com-
" pany's possessions."

To this position it is necessary to demur. It
cannot be admitted that during the last quarter
of a century any considerable improvement has
taken place in the preparatory training of the
Anglo-Indian Judges. On the contrary, it has
been proved by experience that in consequence
of the changes which during that period have
been effected in India in the constitution of the
inferior tribunals, by the more extensive employment as Judges in them of Natives and other uncovenanted functionaries, the opportunities afforded
to the members of the Civil Service, who under
the present system alone are eligible to the higher
judicial offices, of acquiring the necessary qualifica-

tions, have been very considerably decreased. The institution at Haileybury has been in existence for the last forty years, and for a very considerable portion of that period the course of instruction has embraced all the subjects now taught there. It has of necessity followed from the number of subjects studied, that the students exercise a certain degree of selection as to the studies to which they shall more especially devote their attention ; it having been found impracticable, or at all events inexpedient, that a high or even a fair standard of proficiency in *all* should be absolutely required. To the majority of youthful students the study of law is by no means an attractive one; and though perhaps of all others the one most calculated to tend to the efficiency of the future civilian, it has been more generally neglected at Haileybury than any other, and few young civilians arrive in India with more than the merest smattering of legal knowledge.

It is obvious, therefore, that, even as regards a theoretical knowledge of the laws he will be called upon to administer, the Haileybury education in the majority of cases affords a very inadequate preparation to the future Anglo-Indian Judge. Admitting, however, for the sake of argument, that the objects of the institution were fully carried out, and that every civilian was sent out to India with a well-grounded knowledge of the general principles of jurisprudence, it is hardly necessary to observe that but one step (in itself certainly a most important one) would have been attained towards the standard of qualification which is essentially requisite for the successful exercise of the judicial office. It is necessary that the training should be practical as well as theoretical, and that a judicial tone of mind should be framed and habits of judicial investigation acquired before the future Judge can be pronounced qualified to administer the law. What, then, is the nature of the practical training which the Company's Judges undergo previous to being invested with strictly judicial duties? On first arriving in India all Civil Servants are required to study one or more of the native languages, and when reported qualified in this respect for entering upon the duties of the service, are appointed assistants to a collector and magistrate, which functions, we have seen, are everywhere but in Bengal Proper united in the same individual. In Bengal Proper, where the two offices are separate, the duties of the assistants are principally, it is believed, magisterial. For the first year or so the assistant is employed in trying petty misdemeanors under the immediate supervision of his official superior, and in acquiring a knowledge of the revenue system in force. He is then entrusted with the separate charge of a small division of the district to which he belongs, and exercises the full powers of a magistrate both in his judicial capacity and in his capacity of committing officer to the Court. In the present state of the several services, the promotion being now much slower than it used to be, the civilian usually continues in his first office for some five or six years, employed in magisterial investigations and the management of the revenue affairs of the division under his charge. In Bengal Proper, at this period of his service he generally succeeds to a full magistracy, in which he continues perhaps for eight or ten years more, when he is promoted to a collectorate, and, after some years' service in that department, eventually rises to the office of Civil and Session Judge.

In Madras and Bombay there are the subordinate grades of Judgeships, which are attained earlier in the service, and afford certainly some preparation for the more important functions of the superior Courts. In all the Presidencies, however, the duties of the revenue and magisterial functionaries are to a certain extent judicial. The magistrates in all have a certain criminal jurisdiction, and the revenue officers are constantly engaged in investigations partaking in some degree of a judicial character.

It is argued that they thus acquire habits of accurate investigation and a knowledge of the character and habits of the people, and of the various tenures of land, well calculated to fit them for the discharge of the duties more peculiarly appertaining to the judicial office; and by those who uphold the existing system it is contended that by the sort of preparation they receive, the future Judges become really better qualified for their posts than would be the case if the earlier periods of their service had been passed entirely in the Courts.

This argument has had the advantage of all advocates from Sir Thomas Munro downwards, and the system based upon it having been found in many respects a convenient one, its evil effect upon the administration of justice has been left almost entirely out of sight. It might be supposed, and it is the general impression in India, that in the criminal department at all events the duties of the magistracy afford a good preparation for the functions of Criminal Judge. It seems not unnatural to infer that a man who has passed several years in adjudicating upon offences up to a certain limit, and in his capacity of committing officer in investigating, and preparing for trial, cases of a more serious kind, should after a time become well qualified for discharging the functions of the superior tribunal; and yet it is in the criminal department that, to judge from the printed reports, the deficiencies of training and the want of habits of accurate investigation are most palpably apparent. It is impossible to peruse the records of the most serious criminal cases which are referred for the final judgment of the Sudder Courts without being struck by the utter absence of a judicial tone of mind on the part of the Judge presiding at the trial which these records very frequently display. We find conclusions arrived at altogether unsupported by the evidence upon which they are founded, and questions omitted upon most important points,—the result of the Judge having arrived at a conclusion without sufficiently analysing in his own mind whether that conclusion was justified by the premises upon which it was based.

A few of the remarks recorded by the Judges of the Sudder Courts on the trials of criminal cases referred to them, which are to be found in the printed reports, will serve to illustrate the defects referred to. For instance, in a case of murder, in which one of the principal circumstances adduced to convict the prisoner of the commission of the crime, was the discovery in his house of an ear-ring, which was alleged to have been worn by the deceased (a female child of six years of age) when she was last seen alive, it is observed by one of the Judges of the Sudder Court, on review of the evidence, that a goldsmith " who was named by the prosecutor as " the maker of the ornament in question was not " examined by the Session Judge, although, as it " appears that he denied before the police the fact " which he was called upon to establish, and one " which if proved must have had an important " effect upon the prisoner, it was clearly most im- " portant in justice to the accused that his evidence " should have been taken."

On the same trial it is remarked that the evidence of two witnesses whose testimony was considered by the Session Judge to corroborate that of an alleged accomplice,—the only direct evidence to the murder charged, and who stated that they had seen the prisoner, the first witness (the accomplice), and the deceased child on the day the latter was missed, proceed from a particular stone in the village bazaar to the entrance of the prisoner's house,—was contradictory to the statement of the accomplice, from which it appeared that they went in the first instance to a field in a different direction.

"It is possible," the Sudder Judge observed, "that this discrepancy might have been reconciled "by a more careful examination of the witnesses "referred to; but on this point many obvious "questions have been omitted, and the Court are "left entirely to conjecture in regard to the fact "to which the said witnesses have deposed."

In another case the evidence of certain witnesses who were considered by the Session Judge to prove the fact of a prisoner having delivered up from his house certain articles of stolen property, is pronounced by the Sudder Court to be very vague and contradictory, and not to have been subjected by the Session Judge to any cross-examination, "which," it is pointed out, "was clearly necessary "to reconcile the contradictions which the state- "ments of those witnesses involved"—or "*to expose* "*their worthlessness*" might with propriety have been added; nor was the latter by any means the least probable of the two possible results.

The above may be considered as fair examples of the errors into which judicial officers are constantly

liable to fall, if deficient in that preparatory training which alone can correct the natural proneness
of the human mind to jump at conclusions without
duly considering whether the facts from which it
deduces them are satisfactorily proved.

For this purpose the antecedent employment of
the Indian civilian in the duties of the magistracy
or in the subordinate Courts is in a large proportion
of instances comparatively useless. Beyond the
supervision of the appellate tribunals, which under
the most favorable circumstances must operate but
very imperfectly as a guide to the novice in judicial
investigation, there is no means, under the existing
system, of correcting the erroneous notions which a
young man may imbibe at the commencement of
his career. Many of them may consequently become
inveterate; and loose habits of investigation may
be acquired which no amount of subsequent experience will effectually remove.

Some years ago there was a class of judicial
offices filled from the junior ranks of the Civil
Service, one of whom under the designation of
Register was attached to each Zillah Court, and was
empowered to try civil and criminal cases referred
to him by the Zillah Judge. Their duties, indeed,
were entirely judicial, and their official designation,
the origin of which we have been unable to trace,
and which to English ideas is as ungrammatical as
it was inapplicable, was altogether a misnomer.
These offices to a certain extent afforded a school

for training to the judicial branch of the Civil Service. But in them there was the evil that the education of the Judges was conducted at the expense of the suitors, instead of having been acquired previous to their being called upon to administer the law; and as the only check upon them was the supervision of the appellate tribunals, as schools for training they were open in some respects to the same objections which apply to the magistracy and the present subordinate Courts in the Presidencies of Madras and Bombay. The objection to such a system is forcibly put by Mr. Cameron, one of the late Indian Law Commissioners, in a minute recorded by him on the means of educating for judicial functions, in which he observes that a person "whose business it is to hear " and decide small causes does indeed acquire " actual experience; but he acquires it at the " expense of the unfortunate suitors, on whom his " education inflicts all the misery resulting, not " only from injustice, but from injustice aggravated " by the fallacious promise of justice. Moreover, " as small causes are generally the causes of the " poor, and large causes the causes of the rich, " the unseemly spectacle is exhibited of a Judge " having to adjudicate *well* the rights of the great " and opulent by adjudicating *well* or *ill* the rights " of the vulgar."

These officers, however, have for several years been abolished, and notwithstanding the objections

urged in the foregoing remarks to Courts of Small
Causes being constituted into schools for the training of judicial officers, and to the suitors in them
being exposed to the evil effects of judicial inexperience on the part of the presiding Judge, their
abolition appears to have been an error, in the
absence of any better system of training for the
more important duties of the superior Courts.

We say that " in the absence of a better system "
the abolition of the Registerships appears to have
been a mistake; but at the same time it is sufficiently apparent that a much more useful system of
training might very readily be devised; and at the
time the abolition of those appointments in the
Madras Presidency was resolved on, (for *there* they
were continued as late as 1843,) the Government of
India had before it the sketch of a system of judicial
training, prepared by the Indian Law Commissioners,
well adapted for meeting the exigencies of the
public service, and for rendering the future Judges
of the superior Courts qualified for their posts.
Upon what grounds the plan proposed by the Law
Commissioners was rejected by the authorities it is
difficult to understand. That it has been rejected,
or at all events altogether unattended to, would
seem to be apparent from the length of time which
has passed since it was proposed, the letter of the
Law Commissioners recommending its adoption
being dated so far back as the 2nd July, 1842.

In this letter, which principally adverts to the

legal training necessary for those members of the Civil Service destined for the judicial branch of it, the Law Commissioners premise their suggestions by observing that they advocated, " not those mea-" sures which abstractedly they should consider " the best, but such as they believed would be " found the most effectual, consistently with a due " regard to the patronage vested in the Honorable " East India Company."

This reservation, which evidently pointed at the existing restriction of the higher judicial appointments to the ranks of the Civil Service, we cannot but think was altogether unnecessary; and it appears to us, for reasons which will be stated presently, that the Law Commissioners might with perfect propriety have pronounced the plan proposed by them as abstractedly the best which, having reference to the circumstances of India, it was possible to suggest. It has frequently been argued that the Courts would be much better administered if the Civil Servants of the Company were excluded from judicial employment, and the seats on the bench of the higher Courts of each district in the Mofussil were filled by English barristers sent out from England for the purpose, as is done in the case of the Crown Courts at the three Presidency towns; and it has been contended that the want of local knowledge of the character and languages of the people, which Judges so appointed would necessarily experience during the earlier period of their career,

D

would be amply compensated by the larger amount of legal knowledge and judicial aptitude they would bring to the performance of their functions.

From this position we must most unequivocally dissent. Independently of the difficulty which very often would be experienced of inducing English barristers of superior professional attainments to accept the offices referred to — (and it is sufficiently notorious that the Judges of the Supreme Court, highly paid as they are, and highly pensioned on retirement, in comparison with the duties they are called upon to perform, are not unfrequently persons of by no means first-rate qualifications)— it has been proved by experience that as a general rule no Judge, however trained in legal studies, if ignorant of the language in which the business of the Court is conducted, would be enabled to administer justice satisfactorily in the Mofussil Courts; and this alone, it is conceived, would be an insuperable objection to the employment in them as Judges of English barristers, unfitted by a previous preparation to communicate freely with the parties and witnesses coming before the Court. In the Supreme Courts this evil must be often felt, though probably in a far less degree than it would be in the Mofussil, where a Judge is seldom afforded much aid from the ability of the advocates practising before him, and the check upon the venality or ignorance of the interpreter which is afforded by a large concourse of spectators rarely or never exists.

Another arrangement for the better administration of the Courts of Justice which of late years has been very frequently proposed, is that the field for selection should be extended, and that the higher appointments, instead of being confined to the ranks of the covenanted Civil Service, should be opened to those members of the so-called un-covenanted Service and to other European residents who from their knowledge of the languages and of the people, and ascertained qualifications for the performance of high judicial functions, may be considered well fitted to preside in the Courts.

Such an alteration in the patronage of the judicial service would doubtless in some instances be attended with very satisfactory results, and would occasionally afford an opening for the employment in the higher Courts of persons eminently qualified by their talents and experience to preside in them, but who under the existing system are debarred from aspiring to any but the more subordinate posts. For many years, however, it is scarcely to be expected that any large number of persons could be selected from the class referred to;—that is, from the European residents in India not belonging to the covenanted Service of the East India Company, really qualified by training and experience for high judicial office. Selections might occasionally be made from among the pleaders of the Sudder

Courts or from among such of the barristers of the
Supreme Court as had applied themselves to the
study of the vernacular languages, and of the laws
in force in the Company's Courts; but for many
years to come such selections could be by no means
numerous, nor would the advantages to be derived
from them sufficiently counterbalance the incon-
veniences that would arise from altering the constitution of the Service, and depriving its members
of those incentives to industry and integrity in the
discharge of their duties which experience has
proved to be the surest warrant for efficiency and
purity in the administration of the Indian Government in its various departments. It is easy to
declaim about class interests and class prejudices,
and the evils of a monopoly which ensures to a
certain set of persons the possession of certain
offices within a certain number of years. Abstractedly it undoubtedly is an evil; and if the administration of justice or of the other departments of
Government were likely to be practically benefited
by the abolition of the monopoly which at present
exists in favor of the Civil Service, it would of
course be out of the question to advocate its retention; but after a careful consideration of the subject
in all its bearings, and especially referring to the
present circumstances of the country and the
character and condition of its inhabitants, and the
non-existence, so to speak, of any public, whereby
the proceedings of the public officers might be

controlled, it seems clear that the very exclusiveness
of the Service has its advantages, far exceeding
any which would be likely to accrue from the
alterations that have been proposed; and that as
a general rule the work may be performed more
efficiently and at a less cost to the State by retain-
ing an exclusive service for the administration of
all important offices, than could be done under a
different arrangement,—provided the members of
that Service be properly trained at the outset for
the duties they are called upon to perform. To
the judicial department especially the advantages
of such an arrangement appear to us most remark-
ably to apply. It is now universally admitted that
Judges should be well-paid officers, and that such
retiring pensions should be provided for them as
may make it worth the while of competent persons
to undertake the office. The necessity for liberal
pensions for services rendered in a climate like that
of India is sufficiently obvious to remark, and it is
in regard to the question of retiring pensions that
in point of economy the advantage of having an
exclusive service, the members of which entering
it in early life rise gradually to the higher offices
reserved to it, seems to be most clearly established.

Under a covenant entered into on his appointment every member of the Civil Service becomes
entitled, after the completion of twenty-five years'
service, including three years of furlough, to a
pension of £1000 a year, the portion of which

paid by the State does not on the average exceed much above £300 a year, while the remainder is made up by subscriptions of the parties to the covenant on a kind of mutual assurance system, each individual being required to subscribe 4 per cent. on his salary from his admission into the Service, and to have made up by his accumulated subscriptions with interest, which at the rate of 6 per cent. is allowed by the State, an amount equal to half the value of the annuity when the pension is taken, all the subscriptions of those who die in the service going towards the payment of the other half.

In this way, at a cost to the State comparatively trifling, a liberal pension is provided, with the arrangements for which the admission into the higher appointments of the Service of persons altogether unconnected with it would be found most materially to interfere, and, keeping in view the principle that high judicial appointments should not only be well paid but well pensioned likewise, would entail on the Government much additional expense.

For these reasons we consider that no system could be devised better adapted to the circumstances of the country than that of a trained service vested with such exclusive privileges as may render admission into it an object of competition, and may afford to its members sufficient incitement to make themselves thoroughly efficient in the discharge of their duties; and therefore we are of opinion that the measures proposed by the Indian Law Commissioners in the communication to which we have already referred might with justice have been pronounced by them to be such as would be found the most effectual, not only " with a due regard to the " patronage vested in the Honorable East India " Company," but with a due regard to the far more important interests involved in the establishment of an efficient system for the administration of justice to the population of the country over which that Company bears rule.

But while we advocate the retention of the monopoly at present vested in the Indian Civil Service, it will be apparent, from the facts stated and the considerations urged in the preceding pages, that we are at the same time fully alive to the necessity for an improvement in the system under which the members of the Service are trained and selected for the judicial branch of it; and we shall now briefly describe the leading features of the plan proposed by the Law Commissioners, which, as we have already observed, appears to us to be under all circumstances the most practicable and the best adapted for the attainment of the object in view.

It was proposed, then, by the Law Commissioners that the field for selection for admission into the Service should, as far as practicable, be extended, and that, by adopting the principle of competition from among a large body of candidates, a sufficient number of young men possessing superior talents and acquirements should be secured.

With this view they recommended that all appointments by the Directors of the East India Company should be made in the first instance to the general Service, and that the candidates for the Civil Service should be selected at an examination involving a high test of attainments, the appointments to that Service being bestowed according to priority on the examiners' lists.

It is to be observed the scheme proposed was merely an enlargement of one of those named on the occasion of the renewal of the present Charter in 1832 and 1833, when the plan of nominating four candidates for every appointment available was frequently urged, but without success.

Having thus advocated the principle of competition in the selection for admission in the Service, the Commissioners proceeded to sketch out the course of instruction which they deemed it advisable that the successful candidates should undergo in England, previous to their departure for the scene of their future labours. Haileybury, it is evident, found no favour with them whatever, and their recommendation, that during the probationary course in England the future Civil Servants should be permitted to choose their own places of instruction, of necessity involved the abolition of the Haileybury institution.

The course of study was to embrace " History

" in general, and the History of India in particular;
" Political Economy ; Moral and Political Philo-
" sophy ; and Jurisprudence, especially that branch
" of it which relates to the Conflict of Laws." We
should be disposed to add another branch of it of
still greater importance, viz. that which relates to
the Rules and Principles of Evidence.

The progress of the students was to be ascertained by annual examinations, the course of study
extending through a period of three years, at the
conclusion of which the candidate was to be rejected
if unable to attain a certain fixed standard of qualification, or in the event of his general conduct and
character being found to be unsatisfactory. The
study of the Oriental languages was to form no
part of the course of instruction proposed.

On their arrival in India the attention of the
Civil Servants was to be principally directed to the
study of the vernacular languages, proficiency in
two of which was to be required.

Their professional studies were then to assume a
local character, and by attendance at courses of
lectures to be delivered on the enactments in force
in the Presidency to which they belonged, on the
printed reports of cases decided by Her Majesty's
and the Company's Superior Courts, and on the
principles of the Hindu and Mahomedan Laws,
they were to complete the theoretical portion of
their legal education ; and as a means of obtaining
some practical knowledge of the administration of

justice, they were at the same time to be required occasionally to attend the trials, civil and criminal, in the Courts of Judicature.

Their progress in this, as in the other parts of their probationary course, was to be tested by periodical examinations; and after passing a further test of qualifications, they were to be declared qualified for employment in the public service.

Upon this point the Law Commissioners were agreed as to the course of preparation to be undergone by all members of the Service, including those to be selected for the judicial branch of it; but here a difference of opinion arose between Mr. Cameron and his colleagues: the majority of the Commissioners recommended that in the Presidencies of Madras and Bombay, and, if practicable, also in Bengal, every Civil Servant, on being reported qualified to take a part in public business, should be employed for three years as an assistant to a collector and magistrate, with the view of " per-" fecting himself in the languages, and acquiring a " general knowledge of the manners, habits, feelings, " and institutions of the people ;" and that, after the expiration of this period of Mofussil preparation, the ablest and most competent should be selected for employment in the judicial line, in which, after having been once chosen for it, they should be thereafter exclusively retained.

For those so selected the Commissioners unanimously recommended that at least one year should

devoted to a kind of judicial apprenticeship
evious to their appointment to the exercise of
lependent functions, during which period of ap-
enticeship each probationer should be attached
an Official Assessor to a Mofussil Court, super-
ended by a covenanted European Judge, or to
tain civil and criminal Courts subordinate to
Superior Court which they had previously re-
mmended to be established at each Presidency.
It was proposed that in his capacity of Assessor
probationer should sit with the Judge on the
al of cases civil and criminal, attending closely
roughout to the conduct of the cause, and giving
opinion " upon every matter coming for decision,"
ich opinion, however, " should have no legal
effect, and indeed no other effect than such moral
influence as the training and character of the
officer delivering it and the arguments by which
he might support it should produce on the mind
of the Judge."
The Commissioners further proposed that the
ssessors should be occasionally employed in the
inisterial duties now left principally to the ministe-
al officers of the Court, and so obtain an insight
to the practical working of the Court in all its
tails. It was also suggested that they should
occasionally deputed for the purpose of conduct-
g local investigations connected with cases depend-
g before the Judge.
It was pointed out that upon the plan proposed

the probationer, when employed as an Assessor in the trial of cases civil and criminal, would actually go through all the duties of the judicial office, not excepting that of deciding, but that the decisions having no legal weight would, if erroneous, have no evil influence on the suitors or parties before the Court; and that, while thus engaged under the guidance of an experienced officer in the operation of weighing evidence, of applying the principles of the law to the facts which the evidence establishes, and eliciting from the evidence the facts which form a proper basis for the application of the principles of law, he would " derive all the benefits of real experience " without inflicting upon the suitors any of those " evils to which judicial inexperience gives rise."

The point upon which Mr. Cameron dissented from his colleagues had reference to their recommendation that every judicial officer, previous to being set apart for the judicial office, should undergo a preparatory training for three years in the revenue and police departments. This time, Mr. Cameron was of opinion, would be better occupied by the employment of the probationer as an Assessor in a Court. His colleagues considered that " by such " employment in the revenue department as they " contemplated, a young man would acquire a " better command of the native languages, which " he must of necessity be continually using, than " if he were occupied during the same time in the " duty of an Assessor to a Court without any

" obligation, or having any need, to take an active
" part in the proceedings as an interlocutor." It
appeared to them also that "a man whose duties had
" brought him into contact with all classes, and
" had afforded him opportunities of making himself
" acquainted with their manners and habits, their
" ways and forms of dealings and intercourse with
" each other, and the details of their economy
" generally,—who had conversed with them freely,
" and was used to hear them speak without reserve,
" was likely to be better able to deal with a witness
" so as to elicit the truth from him, and to know
" when he had got the truth; better able to esti-
" mate the value of native documents exhibited in
" evidence, and to understand the merits of causes
" turning upon the ordinary transactions and deal-
" ings of Natives among themselves; better able,
" therefore, than one of the same standing who
" had had no opportunities of becoming acquainted
" with the character of the Natives except as it had
" been exhibited by those whom he had had to do
" with only as adverse litigants or as tutored wit-
" nesses, although by his practice in judicial
" business he might have become better versed
" in jurisprudence, and more expert in applying
" its principles and rules."

To the first of the grounds urged in the foregoing
remarks in support of the proposed preparatory
training of all judicial officers in the revenue department, viz. the increased facilities it would afford

for acquiring a thorough command of the native languages, Mr. Cameron replied, that as the official Assessor would be required to express his opinion in all cases in which he might be employed, and would be liable to be consulted by the Judge at any moment during the progress of the case, it seemed to him that the shame of being obliged to confess or of letting it be seen in public that he did not understand what was said would be a very powerful stimulus to the acquisition of the language in which the proceedings were conducted—such a stimulus, Mr. Cameron added, as he should suppose none but the incorrigibly idle and worthless would disregard.

And with reference to the comparison instituted by the majority of the Commissioners as to the relative facilities which the two systems would afford for acquiring such a knowledge of the Natives, and of their habits and character, as would be necessary for the successful performance of the judicial office, Mr. Cameron remarked, that " if the question were " simply which of these two men was likely to know " most of the Natives generally, he should not pro- " bably have much difficulty in giving the same " answer as his colleagues would give; but that, " as the question was, which of these two men was " likely to know most of the Natives considered as " adverse litigants and tutored witnesses," to that question he was compelled to answer,—" he who " had devoted his time to the study of them in that

" particular character under the advice and cor-
" rection of a man who has already acquired ex-
" pertness in the process of examination, and cor-
" rectness in estimating the results."

We have thought it right to state at some length the views propounded on each side of the question, which is by no means a very easy one to decide ; but on one point we are fully prepared to agree with the majority of the Commissioners, viz. in regarding the revenue and police apprenticeship proposed by them as offering facilities for the acquisition of a full command of the native languages incalculably superior to those which would be within the reach of the Assessor when engaged in that capacity in the performance of judicial duties. The acquirement of such a full command of a foreign language as may enable a person taking part in judicial investigations fully to comprehend the various niceties and shades of expression and the colloquial usages of particular terms, whereby the meaning of the deponent may be so materially affected, can only be arrived at by constant colloquial intercourse with the people by whom it is spoken, and to those who have not a natural facility for the acquirement of languages is a matter of no small labour in the outset, and one which can only be satisfactorily got through by the learner being thrown for a time entirely upon his own resources, and compelled by the nature of his duties not only to understand what is addressed to him, but to make himself thoroughly understood. This training, we think, should be undergone previous to the selection of the Civil Servant for employment in the judicial department. It is to be feared that in many instances the considerations urged by Mr. Cameron as furnishing an inducement to the official Assessor to remedy any deficiencies he might experience in his knowledge of the native languages would prove practically inoperative ; and so essential do we consider such a qualification to the efficient discharge of judicial duties, that we would exact from every candidate for judicial employment a thoroughly practical knowledge of at least one vernacular language as a sine-quâ-non for admission into that branch of the Service.

The Law Commissioners very properly concluded their suggestions for placing the judicial establishment upon an efficient footing by recommending that its emoluments should " be so adjusted as to " render it on the whole the most lucrative branch " of the Service."

We have already stated our concurrence in the general principles of the plan proposed. That the principle of competition should to a certain extent be observed in admission into the Service would appear to be incontestible, and that for those who are destined for employment in the judicial branch of it a certain professional training is required, will, we think, scarcely be denied. It is true that on the subject of competition for admission very various opinions have been entertained. It has been argued that the adoption of such a rule would in many instances involve a premature and erroneous decision as to the merits of the competing candidates, and that it by no means follows that those who, as youths of seventeen or eighteen, acquit themselves most creditably at a public examination will prove the most efficient men of business in after life. In support of this argument several instances have been adduced, but nevertheless we believe it to be an unsound one, and that in this case, as in many others, the old saying holds good, that the exceptions serve to prove the rule. We believe that by the adoption of this principle of competition the efficiency of the Service could not fail to be improved, and that of those who in after life would be found to have retrograded from their early promise, the instances would be but few. We are not among those who consider high educational qualifications to be incompatible with practical efficiency in the duties of every-day life ; nor can we subscribe to the doctrine recently propounded by a noble Lord,* whose predilection for military affairs has tended in some degree to warp his judgment on questions of civil government, that book-knowledge is by no means a necessary qualification for those employed in the civil administration of our Indian dependencies. Least of all, when considering the training requisite for the exercise of

* The Earl of Ellenborough.

E

judicial functions, can we admit such a doctrine to apply. In all matters concerned with the administration of justice we are disposed to place our confidence in institutions rather than in individuals, and have but little reliance in the efficiency of that so-called practical common sense, which is supposed by some to make up for ignorance of the rules which should guide all judicial investigations.

At the same time we are fully alive to the necessity of not confining the training of the future Judges to that purely theoretical preparation which books or lectures are calculated to impart. It is most necessary that the Judge's education should be completed by a practical training in the duties for which he is destined; and such, it appears to us, will be most efficiently supplied by the adoption of the plan of Assessors which the Law Commissioners proposed.

It remains for us to offer a few observations upon the training of the uncovenanted officers who preside in the lower Courts. These offices, as we have before stated, are generally filled by either Natives or East Indians, although open to all persons without reference to creed, colour, or caste; and the individuals who fill them, though usually inferior in point of education to their more favoured brethren of the covenanted Service, very frequently have the advantage of the latter in regard to what may be termed more strictly professional attainments. The majority of them have held in the first instance subordinate ministerial offices, or have practised as pleaders in the Courts, and have so acquired a knowledge of the rules of Court practice and procedure, superior in many instances to that possessed by the more highly-paid covenanted Judge. They are naturally also more familiar with the habits and customs of the people, and more competent to estimate the value of the evidence brought before the Courts. In a knowledge of general principles, and in those habits of accurate investigation " which shall trace the doctrine upon " which ordinances rest, and which, as well as a " mere knowledge of positive ordinances, are essen- " tial to judicial excellence," the want in most cases of a liberal education must undoubtedly be much experienced by the class of officers to whom we refer; and it is to the general diffusion of European education, and to the establishment of law classes at each of our Indian Presidencies, that we must look as the only means of improving in this respect the qualifications of the officers who preside in the inferior Courts.

The plan of Assessors recommended by Mr. Cameron might certainly be introduced with advantage in their case, as well as in that of the covenanted European Judge; but to be effectual, it should of course be preceded by a more liberal education than the uncovenanted judicial officers usually undergo.

In one respect the inferior judicial appointments are based upon sounder principles than those which regulate the appointments to the superior Courts.

All District Moonsiffs are required to undergo an examination previous to being permanently appointed to the office, and as the superior appointments of Sudder Ameens and Principal Sudder Ameens are seldom bestowed on persons who have not filled the office of District Moonsiff (the lowest grade of judicial functionaries), it follows that throughout the uncovenanted Judicial Service there is a certain test of professional attainments, which in the covenanted Service does not exist. In the former Service, moreover, the seats on the Bench of Justice are considered to be the prizes of merit and superior qualifications, and not of mere seniority in any particular department of the State.

With the foregoing remarks we must leave the subject for the consideration of those whose duty it will be to decide upon the various questions affecting the welfare of our British Indian Possessions. It has been our object to present an impartial sketch of the existing system, with especial reference to those parts of it in which reform appears to be most urgently required; and if the observations we have offered should lead to further investigation on any points of importance which might otherwise have been overlooked, our purpose in placing them before the public will have been most fully attained.

THE END.

PELHAM RICHARDSON 23 CORNHILL.

Lightning Source UK Ltd.
Milton Keynes UK
UKHW020215030119
334668UK00005B/268/P

9 780332 657103